A bibliography on "English for engineers," for the use of engineering students, practicing engineers, and teachers in schools of engineering, to which are appended brief selected lists of technical books for graduates in civil, electrical, mechanical, and

Wilbur Owen Sypherd

Nabu Public Domain Reprints:

You are holding a reproduction of an original work published before 1923 that is in the public domain in the United States of America, and possibly other countries. You may freely copy and distribute this work as no entity (individual or corporate) has a copyright on the body of the work. This book may contain prior copyright references, and library stamps (as most of these works were scanned from library copies). These have been scanned and retained as part of the historical artifact.

This book may have occasional imperfections such as missing or blurred pages, poor pictures, errant marks, etc. that were either part of the original artifact, or were introduced by the scanning process. We believe this work is culturally important, and despite the imperfections, have elected to bring it back into print as part of our continuing commitment to the preservation of printed works worldwide. We appreciate your understanding of the imperfections in the preservation process, and hope you enjoy this valuable book.

A BIBLIOGRAPHY
ON
"ENGLISH FOR ENGINEERS"

FOR THE USE OF ENGINEERING STUDENTS,
PRACTICING ENGINEERS, AND TEACHERS
IN SCHOOLS OF ENGINEERING

TO WHICH ARE APPENDED BRIEF SELECTED LISTS OF
TECHNICAL BOOKS FOR GRADUATES IN CIVIL,
ELECTRICAL, MECHANICAL, AND CHEM-
ICAL ENGINEERING

PREPARED BY
WILBUR OWEN SYPHERD
PROFESSOR OF ENGLISH IN DELAWARE COLLEGE

SCOTT, FORESMAN AND COMPANY
CHICAGO   NEW YORK

COPYRIGHT 1916
BY SCOTT, FORESMAN AND COMPANY

PREFACE

This bibliography is an outgrowth from the editor's experience in the teaching of English to engineering students and from his association with teachers of engineering and with graduate engineers. Although it does not pretend to be an exhaustive list of books and articles on the subjects specified, it does include practically everything that the editor could find on the limited subject of "English for Engineers." It is intended to offer to those who may be interested in one or another of the provinces covered, a reasonably ample list of references to books and articles published before January, 1916. Some of these references will appeal only to teachers of English in engineering schools; others will interest mainly students in engineering; others will be of practical service particularly to young practicing engineers; still others, it is hoped, may be of some import to all of these classes. At the suggestion of practicing engineers, some scattered references to "specific clauses" in Specifications have been inserted in division E of section 8, part C, p. 41, in the hope that they may supplement helpfully the material listed in division A of this section. Teachers of engineering have likewise urged the inclusion of the material in the Appendix on the ground that such brief lists will be of great service to engineers just out of college. I should be grateful to users of the bibliography for suggestions leading toward its betterment.

For their generous encouragement and aid in the preparation of this bibliography, I am greatly indebted to my colleagues Professors Koerber, M. vanG. Smith, Preston, and Whittier, to Professor M. S. Whitaker of Columbia University, to Mr. E. H. McClelland, Technology Librarian of the Carnegie Library of Pittsburgh, and to Mr. Jay M. Whitham and other practicing engineers.

May, 1916   W. O. S.

CONTENTS

		PAGE
A	THE IMPORTANCE OF GOOD ENGLISH TO THE PRACTICING ENGINEER	7
B	THE TEACHING OF ENGLISH TO ENGINEERING STUDENTS	9
C	THE COMPOSITION OF ENGINEERING PAPERS	11
	1 GENERAL DISCUSSIONS	11
	(a) Books	11
	(b) Articles	11
	2 MECHANICAL DETAILS	13
	3 USE OF WORDS AND TECHNICAL TERMS	15
	4 THE WRITING OF THESES	17
	5 BUSINESS CORRESPONDENCE	19
	6 REPORTS	21
	7 JOURNALISM	23
	8 SPECIFICATIONS AND CONTRACTS	25
	(a) General	25
	(1) Books	25
	(2) Articles	27
	(b) Clearness	31
	(c) Fairness	33
	(d) Special Articles on the Writing of Contracts	37
	(e) Specific Clauses in Specifications	41
	(1) Civil Engineering	41
	(2) Electrical Engineering	43
	(3) Mechanical Engineering	45
APPENDIX		47
	THE ENGINEER'S LIBRARY	47
	1 MISCELLANEOUS	47
	2 CIVIL ENGINEERING	49
	3 ELECTRICAL ENGINEERING	53
	4 MECHANICAL ENGINEERING	57
	5 CHEMICAL ENGINEERING	59
	6 VALUATION OF PUBLIC UTILITIES	63

A BIBLIOGRAPHY ON "ENGLISH FOR ENGINEERS"

A THE IMPORTANCE OF GOOD ENGLISH TO THE PRACTICING ENGINEER

Breitenbach, *The Value of English to the Practicing Engineer*, Ann Arbor, 1908.

Cassier's Magazine, August, 1912, p. 161.

Clark, John J., *Proc. Soc. Prom. Engr. Educ.*, 18, pp. 333-357.

Clark, John J., *Bull. Soc. Prom. Engr. Educ.*, 1. 3. 189, 190.

Electric Journal, 3. 4. 186.

Ennis, W. D., *Engineering Magazine*, May, 1908, pp. 180-184.

Gherardi, Bancroft, Jr., *Proc. Soc. Prom. Engr. Educ.*, 11, p. 294.

Harrington, J. L., *The Value of English to the Technical Man*, Kansas City, Mo.

Hayford, John F., *Proc. Soc. Prom. Engr. Educ.*, 14, pp. 198-233.

Henshaw, F. V., *Electrical World*, 51. 6. 305-306.

Hollis, Ira N., *Clarkson Bulletin*, 7. 1. 10.

Kennedy, Julian, *Yale Alumni Weekly*, 9. 39. 391.

Kent, William, *Proc. Soc. Prom. Engr. Educ.*, 15, p. 91.

Kerr, W. C., *Humphreys' Lecture Notes on Some of the Business Features of Engineering Practice*, p. 13.

Kurtz, Benjamin P., *The Canadian Engineer*, 26, p. 697.

Ledoux, J. W., *Engineering News*, 67. 11. 492.

Power, 29, p. 251.

Rickard, T. A., *Mining and Scientific Press*, 101. 8. 235.

Strange, W. W., *Mining and Scientific Press*, Nov. 13, 1909, p. 668.

Stratton, S. W., *Clarkson Bulletin*, 6. 1. 6, 7.

Waddell, J. A. L., *Engineering News*, 52, p. 157.

Warman, P. C., *A Plea for Better English in Science*, Washington, 1910. See also *Science*, 18. 461. 563-568.

Wiley, H. W., *Science*, Nov. 28, 1902, p. 845.

Williams, Gardner S., *Trans. Amer. Soc. Civil Engineers*, 57, p. 156.

B THE TEACHING OF ENGLISH TO ENGINEERING STUDENTS

Coöperative Courses in English for Engineering Students. C. W. Park. *Bull. Soc. Prom. Engr. Educ.* 5. 9. 30-37. 1915.[1]

Courses in English in Our Technical Schools. J. M. Telleen. *Proc. Soc. Prom. Engr. Educ.*, 16 pp. 61-73. 1908.

English at the Institute of Technology. H. L. Seaver. *The Nation*, 85, pp. 586, 587. 1907.

English for Technical Students. C. S Northup. *The Sibley Journal of Engineering*, 28, pp. 348-353.

Preparation of Written Papers in Schools of Engineering. F. N. Raymond. *Proc Soc. Prom Engr. Educ*, 19, pp. 48-54. 1911. Discussion, 54-90.

Results of an Experiment in Teaching Freshman English. William Kent. *Proc. Soc. Prom. Engr. Educ.*, 16; pp. 74-97. 1908.

---

[1] This sequence of numbers indicates, throughout volume, number, page or pages, year.

Teaching English in the Engineering School at Tufts College. S. C. Earle. *Proc. Soc. Prom. Engr. Educ.*, 19, pp. 33-47. 1911.

Teaching English in a Scientific School. A. T. Robinson. *Science*, N. S., 30. 776. 657-664. 1909.

C THE COMPOSITION OF ENGINEERING PAPERS

1 GENERAL DISCUSSIONS

(a) Books

Good Engineering Literature. Harwood Frost. Chicago Book Company.

Guide to Technical Writing. T. A. Rickard. San Francisco, 1908.

Handbook of English for Engineers. W. O. Sypherd. Scott, Foresman and Company, 1913.

Manual of Style. University of Chicago Press. New Edition, Revised and Enlarged.

Notes on the Composition of Scientific Papers. T. C. Allbutt. London and New York, 1905.

Theory and Practice of Technical Writing. S. C. Earle. The Macmillan Company, 1911.

(b) Articles

Engineering English. Harry O'Brien. *Engineering News*, 70. 19. 914, 915. 1913.

How to Become an Effective Public Speaker. *Engineering Record*, 73. 10. 331. 1916.

Making of a Technical Book. R. K. Meade. *The Chemical Engineer*, 8. 6. 225-230. 1908.

Making of Literature for Engineers. C. W. Baker. *Engineering News*, 59, pp. 429-431. 1908.

On Engineering English. J. M. Telleen. *Bull. Soc. Prom. Engr. Educ*, 4. 5. 30, 31. 1914.

Plain Writing. George Otis Smith. *Mining and Scientific Press.* Nov. 27, 1915, pp. 827, 828.

Technical Writing. S. C. Earle. *The Sibley Journal of Engineering*, 27, pp. 169-173.

2' MECHANICAL DETAILS

Abbreviations Used in Engineering Work. *Engineering Office Systems and Methods.* John P. Davies. 1915. Pp. 509-514. (Terms relating to Transmission Machinery, Piping, Pumping Machinery and Hydraulics, Steam Engineering, Locomotives, Civil Engineering, Mechanical Engineering, Electrical Engineering, Shipping.)

Author and Printer. F. Howard Collins. Frowde. 1905.

Guide to Technical Writing. T. A. Rickard. Pp. 20-39.

Handbook of English for Engineers. W. O. Sypherd. Pp. 63-96.

Handbook of Style in Use at the Riverside Press. Houghton Mifflin Company. 1913.

Manual of Style. Government Printing Office. Washington, 1908.

Manual of Style. University of Chicago Press. New Edition, Revised and Enlarged.

Preliminary Report of the Committee on the Standardization of Technical Nomenclature. *Proc. Soc. Prom. Engr. Educ.*, 23, pp. 349-361. 1915.

Some Notes on the Writing of Compound Technical Terms. C. W. Park. *Bull. Soc. Prom. Engr. Educ.*, 6. 3. 195-205. 1915.

Standard Typography, Terms, Abbreviations, Spelling, etc. Regulations Governing the Form but not the Substance of Specifications, Standard Methods of Tests, etc. Year Book, 1913, *American Society for Testing Materials*, pp. 11-21.

Suggestions to Authors of Papers Submitted for Publication by the United States Geological Survey. George McLane Wood, Editor. Washington, 1909.

3 USE OF WORDS AND TECHNICAL TERMS

Common Verbal Faults. *Suggestions to Authors of Papers Submitted for Publication by the United States Geological Survey*, pp. 38-46.

Compound Technical Terms. D. E. Carpenter. *Bull. Soc. Prom. Engr. Educ.*, 6. 6. 401-405. 1916.

Correct Use of Hardening-Shop Terms. S. N. Brayshaw. *Engineering Magazine*, 41, pp. 968, 969, 1911.

Definitions of Terms Relating to Structural Timber. Year Book, 1913, *American Society for Testing Materials*, pp. 300-303.

Definitions of Terms Used in Engineering Contracting. H. P. Gillette. *Handbook of Cost Data*, second edition, 1910, pp. 7-9.

Definitions of Terms Used in Road Construction. *Proc. Amer. Soc. Civil Engineers*, 40, p. 3010. (See also *Engineering and Contracting*, 43. 12. 278-280.)

Desirable Technical Words. E. E. F. Creighton. *Proc. Amer. Inst. Electrical Engineers*, 30, pp. 83, 84. 1911.

Development of Engineering Words. J. M. Telleen. *Bull. Soc. Prom. Engr. Educ.*, 6. 5. 325-331. 1916.

Latin Terms Used in Legal Discussions. A. B. Haring. *Engineering Law.* vol 1, pp. 505-508. 1910.

Miscellaneous Faulty Expressions. V. C Alderson. *Bull. Soc. Prom. Engr Educ*, 3. 6 405-418 and 3. 7. 454-466. 1913.

Standard Sewage Works Terms. *Engineering News*, 75. 7. 316, 317; 75. 11. 507. 1916.

Technical Terminology. Report of the Committee on Terminology of the National Electric Light Association, 1915. *Electrical Record*, July, 1915, pp. 36, 37.

Technical Terms in Business Correspondence Relating to Electric Work. *Electrical Review and Western Electrician*, 60. 4. 173. 1912.

Terms and Definitions Provisionally Approved by the British Electrotechnical Committee. *Journal of the Institution of Electrical Engineers*, 52, pp. 593-608. 1914.

Words in Technical Writing. T. A. Rickard. *A Guide to Technical Writing*, pp. 16-19, 40-107.

4 THE WRITING OF THESES

Choice of Subjects for Thesis Work in Engineering Schools. *Engineering and Contracting*, 35. 18. 529, 530. 1911.

Civil Engineering Theses. C. E. Sherman. *Proc. Soc. Prom. Engr. Educ.*, 21, pp. 169-172. 1913.

Rules for Thesis Work. Department of Civil Engineering. University of California Press.

Thesis Directions for Students. H. Wade Hibbard. *Proc. Soc. Prom. Engr. Educ.*, 21, pp. 129-168. 1913.

5 Business Correspondence

Business Correspondence. *Business Man's Library*, vol. 2, 1907.

Choice of Words in Business Letters. *System*, August, 1914, pp. 194, 195.

Effective Business Letters. E. H. Gardner. Student's Edition. Ronald Press. 1915.

Filing of Correspondence in a Manufacturing Business. Sterling H. Bunnell. *Engineering Magazine,* 34, pp. 479-482. 1907.

Form Letters and Follow-Up Systems. Volume 102, Series I. C. S. Books. International Text Book Company.

Handbook of Business English. Hotchkiss and Kilduff. New York University Book Store, 1915.

Handbook of English for Engineers. W. O. Sypherd. Pp. 97-131.

Letters That Make Good. American Business Book Company, 1915.

Making Letters Pay. E. H. Schulze. *Advertising and Selling*, December, 1913, pp. 19, 50-52; January, 1914, pp. 24, 56, 57; February, 1914, pp. 24, 81, 82; March, 1914, pp. 20, 69, 70; April, 1914, pp. 40, 42-44; May, 1914, pp. 42-44.

Standard Form of Correspondence, etc. Used in Department of Water, San Diego *Engineering and Contracting*, 42. 23. 520, 521. 1914.

Which Letters Do You Write? E. L. Barker. *Judicious Advertising*, 10. pt. 2. 88, 89. 1912.

Why Your Letters Don't Pull. W. W. Loomis. *Advertising and Selling*, February, 1915, pp. 59-63.

Writing Letters in a Business-Like Manner. *Machinery*, 13, p. 619. 1907.

6 Reports

Analysis of Mining Company Reports. A. H. Sawyer. *Engineering and Mining Journal*, 97. 17. 850-852. 1914.

Common Deficiencies in Public Works Reports. A. N. Johnson. *Engineering Record*, 70. 19. 519, 520. 1914.

Cutting "Lumber" Out of Reports. *Power*, 41. 22. 752. 1915.

Engineer's Annual Report. C. T. McChesney. *Power*, 37. 19. 666. 1913.

Form of Progress Report. *Engineering and Contracting*, 37. 21. 578, 579.

Handbook of English for Engineers. W. O. Sypherd. Pp. 132-188. 1913.

How Can Annual Reports Be Improved? *Engineering Record*, 71. 9. 254. 1915.

Inspector's Report on a Defective Electrical Equipment. *Electrician's Wiring Manual*. Frank F. Sengstock. Pp. 200-207 1914.

Making a Railway Report. C. F. Spears. *Railway Age Gazette*, 48. 8. 395, 396. 1910.

More About Annual and Other Reports. *Engineering Record*, 71. 17. 512, 513. 1915.

Municipal Reports. *Municipal Journal*, 37. 1. 13. 1914.

Preparation of Engineering Reports. E. B. Stephenson. *Engineering News*, 70. 25. 1218, 1219.

Reporting on Public Service Properties. E. P. Roberts. *Proceedings of the Engineers' Club of Philadelphia*, 31, pp. 237-258. 1914.

Scope of Reports of Public Engineering Departments. *Engineering News*, 54. 15. 387, 388. 1905.

Standard Rules for Preparing Diagrams and Plans and for Manuscripts of Reports (Metcalf and Eddy). *Engineering Record*, 64. 6. 154, 155. 1911.

7 Journalism

English in Technical Journalism. *Mining and Scientific Press*, Nov. 28, 1908, p. 718.

Good Engineering Literature. Harwood Frost. Chicago Book Company.

How Can Engineers Best Utilize the Technical Journals? *Engineering and Contracting*, 42. 14. 306-308. 1914.

How to Use the Technical Journal—Indexing. J W. Alvord. *Electric Railway Journal*, 44. 14. 611, 612. 1914.

Length of Technical Papers. R. C. Benner. *Journal of Industrial and Engineering Chemistry*, 2, p. 331. 1910.

List of Subjects for and Instructions for Preparing Technical Papers. *The Mechanical Engineer*, 24, pp. 548, 549. 1909.

Literary Engineering. George A. Wardlaw. *The Sibley Journal of Engineering*, Feb., 1907, pp. 182-195.

Literary Style in Technical Writings. *Engineering News*, 64, Supplement, p. 17. 1910

Making of a Technical Journal. E. J. Mehren. *Engineering Record*, 69. 8. 223, 224. 1914.

Opportunities for Engineers in Writing for Technical Journals. *Engineering and Contracting*, 36. 6. 142, 143. 1911.

Practice of Typography—Correct Composition. Theodore Low De Vinne. New York, 1904.

Relation of the Engineering Graduate to Technical Journalism. E. T. Howson. *The Wisconsin Engineer*, 18. 6. 271-276. 1914.

Some Faults of Engineering Articles. *Engineering and Contracting*, 37. 19. 510, 513, 514. 1912.

Specializing in Technical Writing. *Machinery* (Engineering Edition), 21, p. 98. 1914.

Technical Journalism. Ray Morris. *Railway Age Gazette*, 46. 18. 939-944. 1909.

Writing of Advertisements for Electric Lighting. Terrell Croft. *Wiring of Finished Buildings*. New York, 1915.

Writing for the Press. Robert Luce. 5th edition. Boston, 1907.

Writing for the Technical Paper. *Power*, 32, pt. 2, 1910, pp. 1903, 1904, 2081, 2122, 2242; 33, pp. 205, 465, 566, 651, 652, 850, 851, 926, 927, 966; 34, pp. 66, 107, 108, 148. 1911.

Writing Technical Articles. *Machinery* (Engineering Edition), 18, pp. 924-926. 1912.

8 SPECIFICATIONS AND CONTRACTS

A. GENERAL

(1) Books

Civil Engineering Specifications and Contracts. Richard I. D. Ashbridge. American Technical Society, Chicago, 1914.

Contracts and Specifications. James C. Plant and A. E. Zapf. American School of Correspondence, 1908.

Contracts in Engineering. J. L. Tucker. New York, 1910.

Elements of Specification Writing. R. S. Kirby. New York, 1913.

Engineering and Architectural Jurisprudence. J. C. Wait. New York, 1898.

Engineering Contracts and Specifications. J. B. Johnson. Third edition, revised. New York, 1908.

Engineering Law—Volume 1, The Law of Contract. Alexander Haring. M. C. Clark Publishing Company, 1910.

Law Affecting Engineers. W. Valentine Ball. London, 1909.

Law and Business of Engineering and Contracting. C. E. Fowler. New York, 1909.

Law of Operations Preliminary to Construction in Engineering and Architecture. J. C. Wait. New York, 1900.

Manual of Engineering Specifications and Contracts. S. M. Haupt. Philadelphia, 1878.

Specifications and Contracts. J. A. L. Waddell and John C. Wait. New York, 1908.

Specifications and Contracts. Cyclopedia of Architecture, Carpentry, and Building, volume 1, pp. 207-369, 379-385. American School of Correspondence, Chicago, 1912.

Specifications for Building Works and How to Write Them. Frederic R. Farrow. London, 1898.

(2) Articles

Architect's Specifications for Electrical Work. W. S. Jones. *Electrical World*, 55. 13. 815, 816. 1910.

Copying Specifications. *Engineering Record*, 65. 18. 477. 1912.

Enforcement of Specifications. Charles B. Dudley. *Engineering News*, 58. 1. 2-5. 1907.

Engineering Specifications. Frank F. Fowle. *Proc. Amer. Inst. Electrical Engineers*, 30, pp. 2029-2047. 1911.

General Clauses in Specifications. See
Electrical Lighting Specifications, second edition. E. A. Merrill. Pages 30-32.
Engineering Contracts. J. A. L. Waddell. *Engineering News*, 54. 23. 607-612. 1905.
Schedule of 120 General Clauses. *Engineering News*, 51. 16. 377, 378. 1904.

Instructions to Bidders on Contracts. Jerome Cochran. *Engineering News*, 67. 10. 434-442. 1912.

Preparation of Railway Specifications. O. S. Beyer, Jr. *Proceedings of the Western Railway Club*, 25. 4. 186-200. 1912. (See also *Railway Age Gazette*, 53. 25. 1185, 1186. 1912.)

Preparation of Specifications for the Reclamation Service. *Engineering Record*, 55. 24. 701-702. 1907.

Principles of Specification and Agreement Writing. C. R. Young. *Canadian Engineer*, 22, pp. 271-273, 324-326, 351, 352, 378-380, 436-439, 491-493. 1912. (Also separately printed in pamphlet form.)

Requirements and Theory of the Advertisement or Notice to Bidders on Contracts for Public Works. Jerome Cochran. *Engineering News*, 66. 11. 306, 307. 1911.

Specifications. *Railway Age Gazette*, 53, pp. 1185ff. 1912.

Specifications. Fred S. Sells. *Journal of the Institution of Electrical Engineers*, 49, pp. 199-219. 1912.

Specification Writing. International Library of Technology, 52, pp. 1-58. 1904, 1905.

B CLEARNESS

Arrangement of Specifications. *Cyclopedia of Architecture*, vol. 1, pp. 73, 74.

Business of Contracting, Chapter 3. Ernest McCullough. 1906.

Clear Specifying and the Nova Scotian Steel-Coal Lawsuit. *Engineering News*, 61. 14. 386. 1909.

Criticism of Overhaul and Clearing Clauses in Specifications. *Engineering News*, 51. 14. 330. 1904.

Criticism of Specifications for Steel Forgings. W. R. Webster. *Trans. Amer. Soc. Mechanical Engineers*, 23, pp. 643-653. 1902.

Engineering Specifications. Michael Longbridge. *Mechanical Engineer*, 29. 730. 72-75. 1912.

Engineering Specifications. Suggestions for Their Improvement. Walter S. Timmis. *Iron Age*, 81, pp. 787, 788. 1908.

Faulty Specifications. *Electrical Review and Western Electrician*, 63. 20. 971. 1913.

Government Specifications. An Example of Neglect of Three Efficiency Principles. F. Percival. *Engineering Magazine*, 39, pp. 853-858. 1910.

Language of Specifications. *Cyclopedia of Architecture*, vol. 1, pp. 69, 70.

Loosely Worded and Inaccurate Clauses in Specifications. *Engineering and Contracting*, 32. 18. 376-378. 1909.

Loose Use of the Word "Capacity." *Engineering and Contracting*, 43. 23. 505. 1915.

Ludicrous Wiring Specifications. *Electrical Review and Western Electrician*, 62. 13. 652. 1913.

Specifications for Engineering Material. *Engineering Office Systems and Methods*. J. P. Davies. New York, 1915, pp. 90, 91.

Specification Writing. Thomas M. Rickman. *Transactions of the Royal Institute of British Architects*, vol. 5, new series, pp. 77-85. 1889.

Suggestions for Drawing Specifications for Engineering Work. H. L. Butler. *Engineering and Contracting*, 31. 5. 98-100. 1909.

Vagueness and Indefiniteness in Specifications. *Power*, 35. 12. 409, 410. 1912.

Wording of Specifications. *The Canadian Engineer*, 27. p. 625. 1914.

Words and Phrases Used in Contracts. W. V. Ball. *The Law Affecting Engineers*, pp. 85-88.

Writing of Specifications. H. P. Breitenbach. *Engineering News*, 67. 10. 443-445. 1912.

Writing Specifications. Leon Lewis. *Power*, 39. 15. 528, 529. 1914.

C FAIRNESS

Approximate Estimates. *Engineering Record*, 57. 8. 220, 221. 1908.

City Contracts and Specifications. *Engineering Record*, 64. 21. 604, 605. 1911.

Contractor's View of City Contracts and Specifications. C. A. Crane. *Engineering News*, 66. 21. 619. 1911.

Contracts and Specifications from the Standpoint of the Contractor. *The Canadian Engineer*, 26, pp. 156-159. 1914.

Contracts with Special Relation to Structural Steel Work. *Engineering Record*, 61. 7. 201, 202. 1910.

Engineer's Contracts and Specifications from a Contractor's Point of View. J. W. Rollins. *Engineering News*, 58. 14. 356-361. 1907.

Example of Specifications Unfair to the Contractor. *Engineering News*, 62. 25. 677. 1909.

How to Draw Specifications, etc. *Engineering News*, 54, 23. 602. 1905.

Importance of Considering the Contractor in Drawing Specifications. *Engineering Record*, 52. 10. 251, 252. 1905.

Legal Criticism of Government Specifications. *Engineering Record*, 53. 9. 244-246; 53. 12. 383, 384, 409, 410. 1906.

Loose Specifications and Dishonest Contracts. *Engineering News*, 60. 14. 368. 1908.

Precarious Expedients in Engineering Practice. John Hawkesworth. *Trans. Amer. Soc. Civil Engineers*, 67, pp. 32-60. 1910.

Relation Between Engineers and Contractors on Highway Work. Onward Bates. *Engineering Record*, 64. 24. 678-680. 1911.

Relations of Engineers and Contractors. D. L. Hough. *Engineering Record*, 64. 23. 644-647. 1911.

Responsibility of the Engineering Profession for the Conduct of Public Contracts. Cassius E. Gillette. *Engineering News*, 57. 22. 587-589. 1907.

Square Deal in Specifications. *Engineering Record*, 55. 15. 454. 1907.

D SPECIAL ARTICLES ON THE WRITING OF CONTRACTS

Agreements for Building Contracts. W. B. Bamford. *Trans. Amer. Soc. Civil Engineers*, 67, pp. 438-552. 1910.

Chief Engineer as Interpreter and Arbitrator. Alex. Simpson, Jr. *Proceedings of the Engineers' Club of Philadelphia*, 28, pp. 109-125.

Contracts for Public Lighting. *Engineering Record*, 59. 21. 646. 1909.

Contracts for Public Works. Report on a Standard Form. *Engineering Record*, 67. 6. 148. 1913.

Court Decision as to Damages for a Contractor's Delay. *Engineering News*, 55. 12. 323. 1906.

Decision on Appeal in the Manhattan Bridge Contract Case. *Engineering News*, 55. 5. 120, 121, 128. 1906.

Deduction of Liquidated Damages for Delay. William B. King. *Engineering Record*, 66. 24. 657, 658. 1912.

Engineer's Fault: A Discussion of Specifications, Contracts, and Law Suits. J. C. Wait. *Engineering News*, 53. 23. 594-597. 1905.

Engineer and the Law. *Engineering and Contracting*, 42. 24. 551, 552. 1914.

Estimated Quantities. *Engineering Record*, 61. 10. 289. 1910.

Form of Contract Adopted and Recommended for General Use by the American Institute of Architects and the National Association of Builders. Merrill. *Electrical Lighting Specifications*, pp. 204-213.

Judicial Interpretation of a Reinforced Concrete Building Contract. *Engineering Record*, 64. 9. 246, 247. 1911.

Law of Contracts. A. A. Aegerter. *Journal of the Association of Engineering Societies*, 52, pp. 311-319 1914.

Legal Effect and Construction of a Contract for Large Works. *Engineering* (London), 82, pp. 479-483. 1906.

List of Articles and Books Relating to Building Agreements. Prepared by W. B. Bamford. *Trans. Amer. Soc. Civil Engineers*, 67, pp. 442-444. 1910.

Penalty Clause in Engineering Contracts. W. Valentine Ball. *Engineering Magazine*, 26. 5. 674-681. 1904.

Penalty Clause in Engineering Contracts. *Engineering News*, 50. 12. 284. 1904.

Relations Between Engineer and Contractor. *Engineering Record*, 66. 3. 72-74. 1912.

Responsibility for Contracting Delays. *Engineering Record*, 66. 21. 561. 1912.

Some Contractual Features of Road Improvements. *Engineering Record*, 62. 18. 478, 479. 1910.

Some Economic Features of Specifications. *Engineering and Contracting*, 38. 2. 29, 30.

Special Representations in Specifications Control General Cautionary Clauses. *Engineering Record*, 69. 18. 510, 511. 1914.

Time Limit to Contracts. *Engineering Record*, 57. 13. 387, 388. 1908.

Time Penalties on Contracts. George A. King. *Engineering Record*, 58. 14. 383-385. 1908.

E SPECIFIC CLAUSES IN SPECIFICATIONS

(1) Civil Engineering

[See references to books and articles (general) on pages 25, 27, 29.]

Checking-List for Specifications and Estimates for Reference with Sweet's Catalogue of Building Construction, third edition, rewritten and enlarged. *Sweet's Catalogue*, 1915, pp. 1-71.

General Specifications for Concrete and Reinforced Concrete. Jerome Cochran. D. Van Nostrand Company, 1913. Bibliographies, pp. 17ff., 47ff., 74ff., 95ff., 133ff., 147ff., 162ff., 244ff.

General Specifications for Steel Railroad Bridges and Viaducts. Revised edition. Theodore Cooper. New York.

Practical System for Writing Specifications for Buildings. W. Frank Bower. New York.

Report on Uniform Specifications for Buildings. W. B. Bamford. *Journal of the American Society of Engineering Contractors*, March, 1911, pp. 169-198.

Sewer Specifications Clay Products Publicity Bureau, Kansas City, Missouri, 1911.

Specifications for Concrete Bridges. Wilbur J. Watson. Engineering News Publishing Co.

Specifications for Engineering Material. *Engineering Office Systems and Methods.* John P. Davies. New York, 1915. Pp. 89-132.

Specifications for Steel Bridges. J. A. L. Waddell. Wiley & Sons, 1900.

Specifications for Street Roadway Pavements S. Whinery. Second edition. McGraw-Hill Book Co. 1913.

Standard Specifications of the American Society for Testing Materials. *Year Book*, 1914.

Standard Specifications for Structural Steel, Timber, Concrete, and Reinforced Concrete. J. C. Ostrup. McGraw-Hill Book Co. 1911.

(2) Electrical Engineering

[See references to books and articles (general) on pages 25, 27, 29.]

Contract and Specifications for Residence Wiring. Terrell Croft. *Wiring of Finished Buildings*, pp. 88-90. New York, 1915.

Electrical Contracting. Louis J. Auerbacher. Second Edition. New York.

Electrical Lighting Specifications. E. A. Merrill. Second Edition. New York.

Electric Light Wiring. C. E. Knox. New York, 1907.

Electric Wiring Specifications. J. H. Montgomery. Van Nostrand. 1916.

Estimating and Specifications in Electric Wiring. *Electrician's Wiring Manual*, pp. 208-253. P. Sengstock, Chicago, 1914.

Government Specifications for Electrical Apparatus. C. F. Scott. *The Electric Journal*, 7. 2. 157-168. 1910.

New Methods and Specifications for Street Lighting. J. H. Perkins. *Electrical Review and Western Electrician*, 55. 14. 643-645. 1909.

Tentative List of Items in Specifications for Electric Wiring. F. A. Wallace. *Electrical Review and Western Electrician*, 64. 18. 872. 1914.

Specification and Design of Dynamo-Electric Machinery. Miles Walker. Longmans, 1915.

Specifications for Electrical Construction. J. H. Montgomery. George Wahr, Ann Arbor, 1909.

Standardization Rules of the American Institute of Electrical Engineers. Third edition, December, 1912.

Standard Specifications for Incandescent Electric Lamps. Sixth Edition. Circular of the Bureau of Standards, No. 13, 1914.

(3) Mechanical Engineering

[See references to books and articles (general) on pages 25, 27, 29.]

Contracts and Specifications (Elements of Power Station Design). W. B. Gump. *Electrical Review and Western Electrician.* 58. 23. 1174-1176; 59. 4. 171-173. 1911.

Specifications for Engineering Material. John P. Davies. *Engineering Office Systems and Methods,* pp. 90, 91, 107-112, 115-132. New York, 1915.

Steam Power Plants. H. C. Meyer. New York, 1912. Specifications for boilers, 37, 43; Corliss engine, 77; non-condensing engine, 75; piping, 133; steam engines, 68-88; steam turbines, 94; water-tube boilers, 46.

APPENDIX

THE ENGINEER'S LIBRARY

1 Miscellaneous

Architectural Drawing, Designing, and Specifications, Books on—*Catalogue of W. T. Comstock Company.*

Brennan's Handbook—A Compendium of Useful Legal Information for Business Men. New York, 1908.

Business Efficiency, What to Read on. Business Book Bureau, 1912.

Business Management, Problems in. *Industrial Engineering*, 2, pp. 216-218. 1912.

Economics of Contracting. Vol. 1 and Vol. 2 (1915). Daniel J. Hauer. E. H. Baumgartner, Chicago, 1911. (List of Books, vol. 2, pp. 259-269.)

Getting the Most Out of Business. E. St. Elmo Lewis. Ronald Press Company, 1915.

International Technical Index. W. P. Cutter. *Engineering News*, 66, pp. 17, 18, Literary Supplement. September 14, 1911.

Lecture Notes on Business Engineering. A. C. Humphreys. Stevens Institute, 1912.

Military Reading Course for Civilian Engineers. *Engineering News*, 75. 10. 473; 75. 11. 506, 507. 1916.

Printed Engineering Resources. J. Martin Telleen. *Bull. Soc. Prom. Engr. Educ.*, 5. 3. 18-27. 1915. (Also separately printed.)

Publicity Engineering. Walter B. Snow. Boston, Mass.

Salesmanship. A List of Titles of Books Recommended for Salesmen in Report of Committee on Education of Salesmen at Convention of National Electric Association, Chicago, June 2 to 6, 1913.

Scientific Management. Tuck School of Administration and Finance. Hanover, 1912.

Scientific Management. Papers and Discussion in *Proc. Soc. Prom. Engr. Educ.*, 20, part 1, 1912.

Scientific Management. C. B. Thompson. Harvard University Press.

Scientific Management, Books on. *Machinery* (Engr. Ed.), 22. 7. 605. 1916.

Selected List of Books Prepared by the Southern Group of Bell Telephone Companies. *Engineering and Contracting*, 42. 17. 377. 1914.

Technical Books, A List of. *Municipal Engineering*, 32. pp. 232, 306, 380; 33 pp. 14, 96, 175, 335, 397; 34. p. 25.

Technical Books and Journals for Libraries. *Proc. Soc. Prom. Engr. Educ.*, 11, pp. 58-92.

Works Management, Bibliography of. *Factory Organization and Administration*. Hugo Diemer, second edition, pp. 356-370. 1914.

2 CIVIL ENGINEERING

American Civil Engineers' Pocket Book. Merriman. Wiley...$ 5.00

Civil Engineer's Pocket Book. Trautwine. Wiley............ 5.00

Control of Water Parker. Van Nostrand................... 5.00

Design of Highway Bridges. Ketchum. McGraw-Hill....... 4.00

A Bibliography on "English for Engineers"

Elements of Water Bacteriology. Prescott & Winslow. Wiley..$ 1.50

Engineering Mathematics. Steinmetz. McGraw-Hill...... 3.00

Field Engineering (Railroad). Searles and Ives. Wiley.... 3.00

Field Manual for Railroad Engineers. Nagle. Wiley........ 3.00

Highway Engineering. Blanchard and Drowne. (1913) Wiley 4.50

Hydraulic Tables. Williams and Hazen. Wiley.............. 1.50

Maintenance of Way and Structures. Willard. McGraw-Hill.. 4.00

Mechanics of Materials. Merriman. Wiley.............. .... 5.00

Notes on Track. Camp. Wm. Camp, Auburn Park, Chicago.. 4.00

Principles and Practice of Surveying. Vol. I. Elementary. Breed and Hosmer. Wiley..................... .... 3.00

Principles and Practice of Surveying. Vol. II. Higher. Breed and Hosmer. Wiley..................................... 2.50

Principles of Reinforced Concrete Construction. Turneaure and Maurer. Wiley.. 3.50

Public Water Supplies Turneaure and Russell. Wiley...... 5.00

Railroad Curves and Earthwork. Allen: McGraw-Hill....... 3.00

Sewage Disposal. Kinnicutt, Winslow, and Pratt. Wiley.... 3.00

Specifications and Contracts. See pages 25-43.

Steel Structures. Morris. McGraw-Hill............. .... 2 25

Treatise on Concrete. Plain and Reinforced. Taylor and Thompson. Wiley 5.00

Treatise on Hydraulics. Merriman. Wiley.................. 4.00

Treatise on Masonry Construction. Baker. Wiley.......... 5.00

3 ELECTRICAL ENGINEERING

Alternating Current and Alternating Current Machinery. D. C. and J. P. Jackson. Macmillan............................$ 6.00

Alternating Currents. Bedell and Crehore. McGraw-Hill..... 2.50

Alternating Current Motors. McAllister. McGraw-Hill....... 3.00

Alternating Current Transformer. Fleming. D. Van Nostrand. Vol. 1 and Vol. 2, each............................... 5.00

Alternating Current Windings. Kinzbrunner. D. Van Nostrand 1.50

American Handbook for Electrical Engineers. Pender. John Wiley and Sons.. 5.00

Continuous Current Armatures. Kinzbrunner. Van Nostrand 1.50

Direct Current Electrical Engineering. Barr. Macmillan.... 3.25

Dynamo-Electric Machinery. Thompson Spon and Chamberlain Two volumes, each............................. 7.50

Electrical Conductors. Perrine. Van Nostrand.............. 3.50

Electric Circuit Karapetoff. McGraw-Hill.................. 2.00

Electrical Meters. Jansky. McGraw-Hill 2.50

Electrician's Wiring Manual. Sengstock. Popular Electricity Publishing Co., Chicago, 1914.......................... 1.50

Electric Motors. Crocker and Arendt. Van Nostrand........ 2.50

Electric Power Conductors del Mar. Van Nostrand......... 2.00

Electric Transmission of Energy Abbott. Van Nostrand.... 5.00

Elements of Electrical Engineering. Steinmetz. McGraw.... 4.00

A Bibliography on "English for Engineers"

Elements of Electrical Transmission. Ferguson. Macmillan.. $ 3.50

Engineering Mathematics. Steinmetz. McGraw-Hill.. ...... 3.00

Experimental Electrical Engineering. Karapetoff. Wiley.
    Volume 1.. 3.50
    Volume 2.. 2.50

Foster's Electrical Engineer's Handbook Van Nostrand..... 5 00

Illumination and Photometry. Wickenden. McGraw-Hill... 2.00

The Induction Motor. Bailey. McGraw-Hill................. 2.50

Magnetic Circuit. Karapetoff McGraw-Hill................. 2.00

Overhead Electric Power Transmission. Still. McGraw-Hill.. 3.00

Principles of Direct Current Machines. Langsdorf. McGraw-Hill 3.00

Problems in Alternating Current Machinery. Lyon. McGraw-Hill 1.50

Problems in Electrical Engineering Lyon. McGraw-Hill..... 1.50

Specification and Design of Dynamo-Electric Machinery. Walker. Longmans 10.00

Specifications and Contracts. See pages 25-45.

Standard Handbook for Electrical Engineers. McGraw-Hill... 5.00

Storage Battery Engineering. Lyndon. McGraw-Hill........ 4.00

Synchronous Motors and Converters. Blondel. McGraw-Hill.. 3.00

Transformer Practice. Taylor. McGraw-Hill................ 2.50

4 MECHANICAL ENGINEERING

Composition and Heat Treatment of Steel. Lake. McGraw-Hill ....$ 2.50

Engineering Chemistry. Stillmann. Chemical Publishing Co.. 5.00

Experimental Engineering and Manual for Testing. Carpenter. Wiley 6.00

Handbook for Machine Designers and Draftsmen. Halsey. McGraw-Hill 5.00

Heat Engineering. Greene. McGraw-Hill................... 4.00

Heating and Ventilating Buildings. Carpenter. Wiley. 4.00

High-Speed Steel. Becker. McGraw-Hill................... 4.00

Internal Combustion Engines. Streeter. McGraw-Hill....... 4.00

Machine Design. Smith and Marx. Wiley.................. 3.00

Machine Design, Construction, and Drawing. Spooner. Longmans 3.50

Mechanical Engineers' Pocket Book. Kent. Wiley.......... 5.00

Mechanics Applied to Engineering. Goodman. Longmans.... 2.50

Power Plant Testing. Meyer. McGraw-Hill................ 4.00

Specifications and Contracts. See pages 25-45.

Steam Boiler Economy. Kent. Wiley...................... 4.50

Steam Boilers. Miller and Peabody. Wiley................ 3.75

Steam Engine. Creighton. Wiley.......................... 5.00

Steam Engine Theory and Practice. Ripper. Longmans..... 2.50

Steam Power Plant Piping Systems. Morris. McGraw-Hill..$ 5.00

Steam Tables and Diagrams. Marks and Davis. Longmans.. 1.00

Steam Turbines Moyer. Wiley........................... 4.00

Steam Turbines. Stodola. Van Nostrand.................. 5.00

Theory of Heat Engines. Inchley. Longmans.............. 2.25

Thermodynamics. Goodenough. Holt 3.50

Valves and Valve Gears. Furman. Vol. I. Wiley.......... 2.50

Valves and Valve Gears. Furman. Vol. II. Wiley......... 2.00

5 CHEMICAL ENGINEERING

Analysis of Dyestuffs. Green. Lippincott & Co. 1915....... 3.00

By-Products of Coal-Gas Manufacture. Lunge. Scott, Greenwood & Son. 1915...................................... 2.00

Celluloid: Its Manufacture, Applications and Substitutes. Masselon. C. Griffin & Co. 1912........................... 7.50

Cement, Concrete and Bricks. Searle. D. Van Nostrand. 1914 .... 3.00

Chemical Calculations. Ashley. Van Nostrand. 1915........ 2.00

Chemical Technology and Analysis of Oils, Fats and Waxes. Lewkowitsch. Macmillan & Co. 1913-15. 5th Edition. 3 vol. 18.00

Chemistry of Paints and Painting. Church. Seeley, Service & Co. Fourth Edition. Macmillan. 1915................ 2.50

Coal Tar and Ammonia. Lunge. D. Van Nostrand. 1909. Fourth Edition. 2 vol.................................. 15.00

A Bibliography on "English for Engineers"

Commercial Organic Analysis. Allen. P. Blakiston's Sons. 1909-13. Fourth Edition.................................. $ 5.00

Dictionary of Applied Chemistry Thorpe. 5 vol. Longmans. 60.00

Electrochemical Analysis. Smith. Blakiston. 1911......... 2.50

Electro-Metallurgy. Kershaw. Van Nostrand. 1908......... 2.00

Engineering Chemistry. Stillman. Chemical Pub. Co. 1910. Fourth Edition... 5.00

Explosives. Marshall. Blakiston's Sons & Co. 1915........ 8.50

Farbstofftabellen. Schultz. Weidmannsche Buchhandlung. 1914 ....

General and Industrial Organic Chemistry. Molinari. P. Blakiston's Sons. 1913 .... 6.00

Handbook of Sugar Analysis. Browne. Wiley. 1912 .... 6.00

Industrial Chemistry. Rogers & Aubert. D. Van Nostrand Co. 1915... 5.00

Industrial Organic Chemistry. Sadtler. Lippincott Co. 1912. Fourth Edition... 5.00

Lubrication and Lubricants. Archbutt. C. Griffin & Co. 1912. Third Edition... 7.50

Manufacture of Organic Dyestuffs. Wahl. G. Bell & Sons. 1914 .... 1.60

Petroleum. Redwood. C. Griffin & Co. 1913. 3 vol.......... 15.00

Technical Chemists' Handbook. Lunge. Van Nostrand. 1908. 3.50

Technical Gas and Fuel Analysis. White. McGraw-Hill Book Co. 1913.. 2.00

Textile Fibres. Matthews. John Wiley & Sons. 1907......$ 4.00

Volumetric Analysis. Sutton Blakiston. 1911.............. 5.50

Wood Pulp. Cross, Bevan and Sindall. D. Van Nostrand. 1915 2.00

6 Valuation of Public Utilities

Engineering Valuation of Public Utilities and Factories.
Foster. Van Nostrand 3.00

Principles of Depreciation. Saliers. Ronald................ 2.50

Public Utilities. Pond. Bobbs-Merrill...................... 6.00

Regulation, Valuation, and Depreciation of Public Utilities.
Wyer. Sears and Simpson............................. 5.00

Public Utilities. Hayes. Van Nostrand.................... 2.00

Valuation of Public Service Corporations. Whitten. Banks.
2 vol. 11.00